DATE DUE

The Homeplace

The Homeplace

Poems by Marilyn Nelson Waniek

Louisiana State University Press
Baton Rouge and London   1990

99 98 97 96 95 94 93 92 91   5 4 3 2

Designer: Laura Roubique Gleason
Typeface: Aldus
Typesetter: G&S Typesetters, Inc.
Printer and binder: Thomson-Shore, Inc.

Library of Congress Cataloging-in-Publication Data

Waniek, Marilyn Nelson, 1946–
   The homeplace: poems / by Marilyn Nelson Waniek.
      p. cm.
      ISBN 0-8071-1640-8 (alk. paper). — ISBN 0-8071-1641-6 (pbk. alk. paper)
      I. Title.
PS3573.A4795H6   1990
811'.54—dc20

"Annunciation," "Chopin," "The Ballad of Aunt Geneva," and "The Fortunate
Spill" were first published in *Ploughshares.* "High and Haughty" was first published
in *Reaper.* "The House on Moscow Street," "Diverne's House," "To Market,"
"Diverne's Waltz," "Balance," "Chosen," and "Life on the Mississippi" first
appeared in *Southern Review.* The author is grateful to the editors of these
publications.

Publication of this book has been supported by a grant from the National
Endowment for the Arts in Washington, D.C., a federal agency.

The paper in this book meets the guidelines for permanence and durability of the
Committee on Production Guidelines for Book Longevity of the Council on Library
Resources. ∞

For my mother,
Johnnie Mitchell Nelson
(1916–1988)

I just knew
we were going to live
some history.

For my father,
Melvin Nelson, Captain USAF (ret.)
(1917–1966)

Okay, crumb-crushers, listen up:
This is how you shoot stars.

For my children, Jacob and Dora.
And for Roger, who gave them to
me.

HAHAHA YOU AR NEET

Acknowledgments

I want to thank the following people for the help they gave me in my search for family information and stories: my cousins, Annisue Briggs, John Ernest Anderson, and Roy Mitchell; my uncle, Rufus C. Mitchell; genealogists Charlotte Ann Allen and Mary Louise Gossum; Ron Bryant of the Kentucky Historical Society; local historian Phyllis Simmons; and Mrs. Mattie Cheirs. I am greatly indebted to the unpublished memoir written by my great-uncle, Rufus B. Atwood, and to the University of Connecticut for a research grant. A surprised thanks to Robert Hunter, for the photograph of Tuskegee cadets: Bob Hunter is second in line, behind my father. My deepest thanks to the Airmen—to Bert Wilson and Edward Wilson Woodward, Sr.—for so generously taking me back to their love affair with the sky.

Thanks, too, are due the friends who read these poems in manuscript, gave me computer advice, and supported my work in many less tangible ways: Jack Davis, John Gatta, Dave Hankins, Deborah Dancy Muirhead, Don Muirhead, and J. D. O'Hara. A special thanks to Roger Phillips, who showed me my house from the air.

Contents

II Wings

I   *The Homeplace*

Diverne (*ca.* 1845–1915) ⊤ Henry Ashburne Tyler (?)

Rufus Atwood
(slave-name "Pomp")

Harriet Atwood

The House on Moscow Street

It's the ragged source of memory,
a tarpaper-shingled bungalow
whose floors tilt toward the porch,
whose back yard ends abruptly
in a weedy ravine. Nothing special:
a chain of three bedrooms
and a long side porch turned parlor
where my great-grandfather, Pomp, smoked
every evening over the news,
a long sunny kitchen
where Annie, his wife,
measured cornmeal
dreaming through the window
across the ravine and up to Shelby Hill
where she had borne their spirited,
high-yellow brood.

In the middle bedroom's hard,
high antique double bed
the ghost of Aunt Jane,
the laundress
who bought the house in 1872,
though I call with all my voices,
does not appear.
Nor does Pomp's ghost,
with whom one of my cousins believes
she once had a long and intimate
unspoken midnight talk.
He told her, though they'd never met,
that he loved her; promised
her raw widowhood would heal
without leaving a scar.

The conveniences in an enclosed corner
of the slant-floored back side porch
were the first indoor plumbing in town.
Aunt Jane put them in,
incurring the wrath of the woman
who lived in the big house next door.
Aunt Jane left the house
to Annie, whose mother she had known
as a slave on the plantation,
so Annie and Pomp could move their children
into town, down off Shelby Hill.
My grandmother, her brother, and five sisters

watched their faces change slowly
in the oval mirror on the wall outside the door
into teachers' faces, golden with respect.
Here Geneva, the randy sister,
damned their colleges,
daubing her quicksilver breasts
with gifts of perfume.

As much as love,
as much as a visit
to the grave of a known ancestor,
the homeplace moves me not to silence
but to righteous, praise Jesus song:

Oh, catfish and turnip greens,
hot-water cornbread and grits.
Oh, musty, much-underlined Bibles;
generations lost to be found,
to be found.

5

Diverne's House

The house of myth;
the house that shame built;
the house given to Diverne.
The myth of a slave woman
who had to be broken, but bore
two children, neither Negro
nor white. The myth
of their father.

The myth of She Loved Him,
She Loved Herself Not.

Three generations removed
from the finest house on Shelby Hill,
my cousin and I pray for a will,
a manumission paper, a deed,
turning crumbling pages
in a dark room
in the dim county courthouse.

We find names:
Die Viernan.
Die Hammock.
Diverna Matson.
Diverne Atwood.
And from them we decipher
the faint history
of a woman nineteen years a slave.

Her first child was born
three years before freedom,
her second on the threshold
of the Great Jubilation.
She married Alf Hammock
("black," the papers state),
when her first child was nine;
Alf divorced her ten years later.
She'd apparently taken up
with Val Matson, a blacksmith ("black"),
whom she married in 1888.
That same year Val Matson willed
his house to Diverne,
adding a few months later
a bitter codicil
leaving his house to his son,
and Diverne an inheritance

of five
measly dollars.

Nigger, I got me a house
already and two bright-skin childrens,
I don't need your promises nor
your black backside neither,
I had me a man in my life,
can't no mangy halfman scrounge
around up under my skirts, you
can do your own
damn cooking.

Diverne's house
was queen of Shelby Hill.
Where it once stood, we found
a car seat and a lot of used condoms.

To Market

All the long way from Jamaica
in the nightmare
the old folks always told you
would carry you off someday,
you stank of boat-sickness,
your first woman-blood
doubling you over with cramps,
but you hustled anyway
when they told you to,
then teetered, blinded by sunshine,
praise Jesus on dry land again.

From New Orleans you were part of a shipment
of twenty-four new and used slaves.
You heard them call Natchez,
Vicksburg, Rosedale, Memphis, Blytheville,
Dyersburg, Hickman.
With each strange name you lost
two or three holdmates.
The last name you heard
was Columbus, Kentucky.

Given a week to rest,
you washed and replaited your hair,
hemmed the dress
the dealer had thrown
in your lap.
You were three together
in the holding house;
they whispered terrible tales:
Bastard's woman love me better,
the reason Master sold me
away from home.
Master catched me
when I run away north:
the son of the devil
thought he could whip me.
Sold me, instead.

One morning before dawn,
the dealer announced
your next stop: Clinton.
Twelve dusty miles
you marched barefoot,
one ankle raw from the chain.

The dealer rode in front,
high on his broad-backed brown horse,
whistling quietly.
Children ran to see you up close
through splintery split-rail fences;
men and women chopping cotton
straightened up to watch you walk past.

9

Diverne's Waltz

Diverne stands in the kitchen as they dance,
laughing and flirting, on the bare parlor floor.
She's taken up the rug, glad for the chance,
at last, to beat it free of sins outdoors.

Her fancy cakes are popular, her punch
has earned light giggles from Miss Atwood's friends.
She'd struggled at Miss Atwood's back to cinch
that tiny waist. *Miss Atwood look right grand.*

Mister Tyler asks for a water-glass of rye:
he's just enlisted, a drop-out from law school.
She notices something dangerous in his eye:
Crazy damn white man, acting like a fool.

Taking her hands, Henry Tyler gives her a twirl
and off they waltz. He swirls Diverne so fast
her head kerchief unknots itself. He smiles
down at Diverne's embarrassment, and gasps:

They blush! Hearing the whispers from the walls,
he sees men grin. His father shakes his head.
But (*That dark rose . . .*) he dances. *What the hell,
who knows? next week, next month, I could be dead.*

Annunciation

Like holes punched in a tin roof, thinks Diverne.
Up North, night don't mean nothing. Just like day.
She wears good herbs. She prays. She'll never learn
to quiet night's deep silences the way
the African women did: They could bring
the island stars down close. *Up North so dark*
seem like somebody dying. When the work
by which they weighed her worth, in late evening
dragged to its spotless end, she sat outside
and watched the stars. Until one night she dreamed
Posterity appeared, she understood
only that she was here, living, and named
for someone dead. Like Abraham, that night
she saw her children: *Lord, they daddy WHITE?*

Balance

He watch her like a coonhound watch a tree.
What might explain the metamorphosis
he underwent when she paraded by
with tea-cakes, in her fresh and shabby dress?
(As one would carry water from a well—
straight-backed, high-headed, like a diadem,
with careful grace so that no drop will spill—
she balanced, almost brimming, her one name.)

She think she something, stuck-up island bitch.
Chopping wood, hanging laundry on the line,
and tantalizingly within his reach,
she honed his body's yearning to a keen,
sharp point. And on that point she balanced life.
That hoe Diverne think she Marse Tyler's wife.

Life on the Mississippi

The trees paint their reflections
along the mile-wide Mississippi.
River-colored swallows dip
quick breakfasts
from the musical morning air.
Diverne and Miss Atwood hurry
from one tall storefront door
into another. They're buying
a white silk trousseau, white satin slippers,
twenty pounds of heavy flour.

It's Diverne's sixth month,
but she doesn't show.
She's afraid to tell,
to hear the filthy accusations,
to answer the question.
Would Miss Atwood
be ashamed enough
to sell her away?

A steamboat whistle
calls her attention
from Miss Atwood's shoulders,
past the fishing boats,
past the barges, to the people
crowding the deck.
Her people, roped off
in the lifeboat corner,
exchange life-stories
and names,
like long-lost relatives
who might not see each other
for another twenty years.

Diverne, pay attention!
On the railing nearest to her
leans a redhaired white man
smoking a cigar.
He gazes into the heart
of Hickman, Kentucky
then writes something down
in a little yellow book.

Chosen

Diverne wanted to die, that August night
his face hung over hers, a sweating moon.
She wished so hard, she killed part of her heart.

If she had died, her one begotten son,
her life's one light, would never have been born.
Pomp Atwood might have been another man:

born with a single race, another name.
Diverne might not have known the starburst joy
her son would give her. And the man who came

out of a twelve-room house and ran to her
close shack across three yards that night, to leap
onto her cornshuck pallet. Pomp was their

share of the future. And it wasn't rape.
In spite of her raw terror. And his whip.

Intermezzo

Pomp, at the foot of her lacy bed,
warmed Mrs. Rogers' feet
until the master broke in
from his room down the hall
and Diverne jumped up from the floor,
scooped her baby out of bed,
and hied them to the cabin
at the foot of the yard.
When the first son was born,
God rest him, little Pomp
tasted white bread and veal,
chewing and spitting them out,
so the frail, cleft-palate baby
could have something to eat.

Then came the years
of nightmare.
Mrs. Rogers fled,
giving Diverne and her son
to her sister, Mrs. Cowgill,
a wide county over.

But Tyler found them,
home for three weeks
from the ranks
of General Forrest's
ferocious raiders.
He whispered promises—
a house, their freedom—
trying to expiate
in tenderness
what he'd seen and done.
Diverne almost,
almost believed.

He hunted her up again
a few years after the war.
Night Riders roamed freely
all over Kentucky;
she was terrified, at first,
to take his money
and move back to town.

But Pomp
was learning to read
from the Cowgill boys,

and Hickman had a school
for colored children
in the basement
of the C.M.E. church.
Diverne hired a wagon,
packed her 32 years
in a burlap bag,
straightened her shawl,
and lifted her children up.

Johnny Cowgill raced from the house
and into the rutted road
to give Pomp a marble.

Pomp Atwood (1862–1933) ── Annie Parker Atwood (1862–1943)

Ray D.   Blanche   Geneva   Annie   Rosa   Rufus   Mildred

Coal

He made a living selling land and coal
as, when he was a boy, he had been sold:
an honest handshake and a signature;
the cash exchanging hands. He owned a store
across the street from Hickman's Negro school,
and shoveled every day onto its scale
as much pride-bright blackness as it would hold.
He speculated well on real-estate.
He made a living.

With three partners, he formed a business called
The Hickman Joint Stock Company, to sell—
delivered by wagon up and down each street—
the groceries almost half of Hickman ate.
His signature is firm, decisive, bold:
He made a living.

Daughters, 1900

Five daughters, in the slant light on the porch,
are bickering. The eldest has come home
with new truths she can hardly wait to teach.

She lectures them: the younger daughters search
the sky, elbow each others' ribs, and groan.
Five daughters, in the slant light on the porch

and blue-sprigged dresses, like a stand of birch
saplings whose leaves are going yellow-brown
with new truths. They can hardly wait to teach,

themselves, to be called "Ma'am," to march
high-heeled across the hanging bridge to town.
Five daughters. In the slant light on the porch

Pomp lowers his paper for a while, to watch
the beauties he's begotten with his Ann:
these new truths they can hardly wait to teach.

The eldest sniffs, "A lady doesn't scratch."
The third snorts back, "Knock, knock: nobody home."
The fourth concedes, "Well, maybe not in *church* . . ."
Five daughters in the slant light on the porch.

Chopin

It's Sunday evening. Pomp holds the receipts
of all the colored families on the Hill
in his wide lap, and shows which white store cheats
these patrons, who can't read a weekly bill.
His parlor's full of men holding their hats
and women who admire his girls' good hair.
Pomp warns them not to vote for Democrats,
controlling half of Hickman from his chair.
The varying degrees of cheating seen,
he nods toward the piano. Slender, tall,
a Fisk girl passing-white, almost nineteen,
his Blanche folds the piano's paisley shawl
and plays Chopin. And blessed are the meek
who have to buy in white men's stores next week.

20

Upper-ten

Big Annie washed white people's linen.
Ray D. taught the school on the Hill.
Blanche taught the school in the Bottom.
Geneva made meals and kept house.
Annie weighed cotton, accounting
for who picked how much, what was paid
(two hundred pounds bought Mildred's school shoes).
Rosa hired out as a maid.

And Rufus, at fourteen, worked
as a shoe-shine boy
in Will Crother's Barber Shop
at the far end of Main Street.
All the barbers were black;
the customers spat
on the brush-scrubbed floor.

Skullbuster Wright,
the Chief of Police,
swung up to the stand one day
and grinned,
Hi yah, Upper-ten.
Put a shine on my shoes.

Rufus bent forward
beneath the seat
to stash his last tip,
wondering for the hundredth time
why old Skullbuster
called him that.
As he straightened back up,
Chief Wright clapped hard knees
to the sides of his head.

The barber shop silenced
as Rufus pulled back
with a smile on his mouth.
If I scream
he may hit me.
He stopped struggling,
but too late:
already warmth raced
down his leg
and onto the floor.

Chief Wright's laughter
rang back from the mirrors.
Pomp Atwood's only son
was a man.

Alderman

One year the town Republicans
asked Pomp if he would mind
if they put him up for office.
Pomp told them they were kind,
but he had seven children
and a wife he cared about:
He was too young to die—
which he sure would, without a doubt,
if his name stood on that ballot.
Two white men came to call
a few days later at his store,
younger than he, but tall
like he was. They told Pomp he was their brother:
It ain't your fault you had a nigra mother.
They said they'd stand behind him if he ran.

After they left, the local Ku Klux Klan
sent Pomp a message: *Boy, we understand
you need to learn your place.* And Pomp withdrew
because the Klan was wrong: By God, he knew.

Hurrah, Hurrah

A full moon rises
over perfect weather
on a hillside in France.
Surrounded by soft laughter
about men who wear their gas masks
in the open latrine,
Sgt. Atwood checks the wires.

As the Allies push toward Metz
the 325th is encamped in Pont-A-Mousson.
Atwood's in charge of the switchboard
and the lives of his men.

The night explodes
with noise first,
then with light.
One shell has destroyed
generals' communications;
the other, unexploded,
scatters the men into panic.
Only the dead
and Sgt. Atwood
remain at their posts.

Atwood spends three hours
connecting and reconnecting the lines.
Reconnecting because more German shells,
like jealous overseers,
keep undoing his work.

When the ammunitions dump
two blocks away takes a direct hit,
Atwood's knocked off his feet.
But the lines are restored.

The front page of the *Courier*
brings the news home:
LOCAL BOY ARMY HERO.
Pomp's fingers soften the clipping
to blurred words on white velvet,
showing it around town.
MY BOY GOT THE BRONZE STAR.

He sits several hours
in the moonlight one evening,
then writes:
        Take your bonus money
        and buy a dark suit
        to come home in.
        Chief Wright's meeting the trains.
        Keep your uniform in your suitcase.

When Rufus comes
they close the curtains
and lock the doors
before seeing, for the first time,
their son and brother in full glory.

Three days later
a colored soldier
is lynched on Main Street.

Rufus never wears the uniform
again in his life.
A black man in France
wasn't the same
as a black man at home.

The Ballad of Aunt Geneva

Geneva was the wild one.
Geneva was a tart.
Geneva met a blue-eyed boy
and gave away her heart.

Geneva ran a roadhouse.
Geneva wasn't sent
to college like the others:
Pomp's pride her punishment.

She cooked out on the river,
watching the shore slide by,
her lips pursed into hardness,
her deep-set brown eyes dry.

They say she killed a woman
over a good black man
by braining the jealous heifer
with an iron frying pan.

They say, when she was eighty,
she got up late at night
and sneaked her old, white lover in
to make love, and to fight.

First, they heard the tell-tale
singing of the springs,
then Geneva's voice rang out:
I need to buy some things,

So next time, bring more money.
And bring more moxie, too.
I ain't got no time to waste
on limp white mens like you.

Oh yeah? Well, Mister White Man,
it sure might be stone-white,
but my thing's white as it is.
And you know damn well I'm right.

Now listen: take your heart pills
and pay the doctor mind.
If you up and die on me,
I'll whip your white behind.

They tiptoed through the parlor
on heavy, time-slowed feet.
She watched him, from her front door,
walk down the dawnlit street.

Geneva was the wild one.
Geneva was a tart.
Geneva met a blue-eyed boy
and gave away her heart.

Aunt Annie's Prayer

Luke 2:36-37

Her magnified voice reverberates
from the white-splashed red brick walls.
The congregation fanning itself
in sticky mahogany pews
nods, amens, and thanks the Lord.
Above her head and the altar
a hand-painted diptych offers
two alternatives: the blond Jesus
yearning heavenward in Gethsemane;
the dark-eyed Good Shepherd
cradling newborn white lambs.
The junior choir stirs
in its loft on the right;
on the left the senior choir
hums and sways in response.

Praise Jesus. We are here
together again this Sunday.
He bore us through the floods last week;
He kept us dry
in the high place at His side.
He woke us up
to glad daylight this morning;
He cast rays of His pure joy
over our problems and pains.

Still, we don't thank Him
as much as we should.
He brought us through,
and still we don't thank Him.
He fed our souls,
and still we don't thank Him.
He gave us children,
and still we don't thank Him.
He made us new music,
and still we don't thank Him.
He lifted us up,
and still we don't thank Him.
He gave us our dignity,
and still we don't thank Him.
He gave us salvation,
and still we don't thank Him.
He bought our freedom,
and still we don't thank Him.

Lord, he set us free,
and still we don't thank Him.

Father in heaven,
I thank You this morning.
I thank You that You have given us
this hallowed day.
I thank You that You have made us
into this nation of fellowship,
conceived in slavery's deceit
but raised on the breast-milk of truth.

We need You, Lord.
Lend us Your stone strength.
For the burden is heavy
and the highway is steep.
Yes, Lord, sometimes it seems like
we're almost there, almost there,
and the stone rumbles on back down.
So many thousand gone.
Yes, Lord, we need You now
more than ever before.

As You shared our enslavement, Lord,
through your son, Jesus:
when we were heartdead;
when we were woe-begotten, bleeding and whipped:
Be with us again.

I've seen through the cloud,
brothers and sisters;
yes,
I've seen through the cloud
to His welcoming face.

> See through the cloud . . .

Yes, Lord. I've seen
the promise of life.
Let us stand and join our choir
in praise. Thank You, Jesus.

> See through the cloud . . .

I've seen through the cloud.

. . . into the rapture
that shines from His face.
See, by His light,
His beautiful light,
our covenant:
justice and grace.

Praise God.
Thank You, Jesus.
Amen.
Amen.

Ray Diverne Atwood Mitchell —— John Mitchell (?–1946)
(1884–1961)

Johnnie   Rufus

High and Haughty

Ray, almost a spinster, gave up
her dreams of princes to marry
a widowed farmer she'd refused
as a proud, lanky girl.
He was intelligent, kind.
And who would be good enough?

On her husband's farm
near Boley, Oklahoma
she was surprised by love,
like a rainbow umbrella
unfolding over their heads.

New people arrived every week,
having heard of an all-black town
from an incredulous mouth
or a Negro newspaper.
Having heard of her husband.
See that big tree?
If you talk to the man that lives there
he'll loan you enough to get by,
maybe lend you a mule.

They weren't rich,
but John would give away
the drawers on his behind
if Ray didn't stop him.
John, think of the children . . .

She loved John
not because he'd made her
his wife and the mother of two
when she was well past thirty.

She loved John because
early one July evening,
after stopping his car in the road,
wading through a peanut field,
taking off his hat
and handkerchiefing his forehead,
a white man called toward the house:
Mister Mitchell?

And Ray became,
at long last,
a queen.

Black Pioneers

There, we'll put the chickens.
There, I'll build the barn.
We'll plow that prairie grass and grow
peanuts and kaffir-corn.
We'll call your filly Starlight,
and the bay gelding Prince.
You'll have your garden over there
behind a picket fence.
I'll build you a great big smokehouse
and buy you a fine cook-stove.
But, Baby, *first*, let's try the bed . . .
    (CENSORED: They're making love.)

Two-Seater

Johnnie and Rufus before bedtime
in the two-seater
listen to cicadas
and laugh at their father's joke:
> An aeroplane flown by a one-legged pilot
> crashed
> in a colored man's field.
> The pilot crawled out
> without his wooden leg
> and hopped through the cotton
> toward the colored man's house.
> The colored man, rocking
> on the front porch,
> spits his tobacco juice
> and calls out, *Hello, Jesus,*
> *how'd you lose your leg?*
Their mother calls them
from the kitchen doorway;
if they don't go in soon,
she'll make them cut switches.
Nigger thought the pilot was Jesus,
because he could fly!

They laugh again,
then wipe,
pull up their pajamas
and race in to bed.

Juneteenth

With her shiny black-patent sandals
and her Japanese parasol,
and wearing a brand-new Juneteenth dress,
Johnnie's a living doll.

Juneteenth: when the Negro telegraph
reached the last sad slave . . .

It's Boley's second Easter;
the whole town a picnic.
Children run from one church booth
to the next, buying sandwiches,
sweet-potato pie, peach cobbler
with warm, sweaty pennies.

The flame of celebration
ripples like glad news
from one mouth to the next.

These people slipped away
in the middle of the night;
arrived in Boley with nothing
but the rags on their backs.
These carpenters, contractors, cobblers.
These bankers and telephone operators.
These teachers, preachers, and clerks.
These merchants and restaurateurs.
These peanut-growing farmers,
these wives halting the advance of cotton
with flowers in front of their homes.

Johnnie's father tugs one of her plaits,
head-shaking over politics
with the newspaper editor,
who lost his other ear
getting away from a lynch-mob.

Armed Men

Ray teaches at the Boley Baptist School,
a little too far away
to travel safely there and back
by buggy every day.
Some years she lets the children stay
on the farm with their doting father,
but this year they're toeing the line at school,
although keeping them here is a bother.

She has to watch them all the time:
Boley's a Negro town,
and sometimes carloads of white men
drive through, looking around.

Today, for instance, as she'd held
silk yard-goods to her cheek
and smiled at the extravagance,
she'd heard the screen-door creak,
and a young, fair-haired white man
had stalked in. His dismissing eyes
had registered Mr. Oliver's store:
first contemptuous, then surprised.

Mr. Oliver said, *Good morning, Sir,*
one moment, please. Miss Ray,
you look Easter-fine this morning.
Can I cut that silk today?

The white man spat a bad name;
Mr. Oliver prepared to fight.
The white man promised to bring some friends
and shoot up the town tonight.

And now, Ray's children expect her
to let them go out and run
through the twilit streets of Boley,
where each window holds a loaded gun.

The Fortunate Spill

*Note: Traditionally, black-eyed peas are served
on New Year's Eve: each black-eyed pea one eats
brings luck.*

Well! Johnnie thinks. *He has his nerve!*
Crashing this party! What stuck-up conceit!
Passing his induction papers around;
another Negro whose feet never touch the ground.

His name is Melvin Nelson. In his eyes
the black of dreams sparkles with laughing stars.

Johnnie agrees to play. And it defies
all explanation: she forgets five bars!
This cocky, handsome boy? she asks her heart.
For good luck all year, Melvin says, *you've got to fart.*

They eat elbow to elbow, in a crowd
of 1942's gifted black youth.
His tipsy bass-clef voice is much too loud.
Hers trebles nervously: to tell the truth,
she's impressed.

        I'll be a man up in the sky,
he confides. She blurts out, *Hello, Jesus!* And they die
with laughter.

        But the joke catches him off-guard:
he spills the black-eyed peas into her lap.
Oh Lord, he mumbles, but she laughs so hard
both recognize the luck of their mishap.

And I watch from this distant balcony
as they fall for each other, and for me.

II *Wings*

Tuskegee Airfield

For the Tuskegee Airmen

These men,
these proud black men:
our first to touch
their fingers to the sky.

The Germans learned to call them
Die Schwarzen Vogelmenschen.
They called themselves
The Spookwaffe.

Laughing.
And marching to class under officers
whose thin-lipped ambition
was to *wash the niggers out.*

Sitting at attention
for lectures about ailerons, airspeed, altimeters
from boring lieutenants who believed
you monkeys ain't meant to fly.

Oh, there were parties,
cadet-dances, guest appearances
by the Count
and the lovely Lena.

There was the embarrassing
adulation of Negro civilians.
A woman approached my father in a bar
where he was drinking with his buddies.
Hello, Airman. She held out her palm.
Will you tell me my future?

There was that,
like a breath of pure oxygen.
But first
they had to earn wings.

    There was this one instructor
    who was pretty nice.
    I mean, we just sat around
    and *talked* when a flight had gone well.

    But he was from Minnesota,
    and he made us sing
    the Minnesota Fight Song
    before we took off.

If you didn't sing it,
your days were numbered.
"Minnesota, hats off to thee . . ."
That bastard!

One time I had a check-flight
with an instructor from Louisiana.
As we were about to head for base,
he chopped the power.

Force-landing, nigger.
There were trees everywhere I looked.
Except on that little island . . .
I began my approach.

The instructor said, *Pull Up.*
That was an excellent approach.
Real surprised.
But where would you have taken off, wise guy?

I said, *Sir,*
I was ordered
to land the plane.
Not take off.

The instructor grinned.
Boy, if your ass
is as hard as your head,
you'll go far in this world.

Freeman Field

For Edward Wilson Woodward, Captain USAF (ret.)
and the 101 of the 477th

It was a cool evening
in the middle of April.
The 477th, the only Negro
bombadier group in the Air Corps,
had just been transferred
to Freeman Field.

Some of the guys
said they were hungry
and left to find food.
The others went on
playing bridge,
mending socks,
writing letters home.

A few minutes later
the hungry guys came back,
still hungry.
We're under arrest.

The others thought they were kidding.

The next morning
the Base Commander
issued new regulations:
Negro officers were assigned
to the NCO Club;
white officers were assigned
to the Officers' Club.

The Base Commander,
who had deliberately busted
an entire Negro outfit
so he wouldn't have to be
their flight-leader in combat,
was a graduate of West Point.

He issued a statement:
If we do not allow
Negro and white officers to mix,
the accident rate
will go down two
and two-tenths
percent.

Sixty-one Negro officers
were ordered to report
one by one
to his office.
Lieutenant, have you read the regulations?
Sign here if you have read and understood.

Sixty-one Negro officers
refused to sign.
A man of your intelligence
must be able to recognize
the dangers of fraternization.

They refused to sign.
This is an order:
Sign the document.

They refused to sign.
This is a direct order!
You will sign the document!

Six cargo planes were called in;
pilots, navigators, and bombadiers
were shoved on board and flown
to Godman Field, Kentucky.

Across the river
was Fort Knox.
The sixty-one
had grown by now
to one hundred and one
American fliers trained
to fight Nazis.
They were confined
to the BOQ
under guard
of armed MP's.

By night, searchlights watched
every window. By daylight
the men leaned in the windows
to smoke, watching
the German POW's pump gas,
wash windshields
and laugh
at the motorpool
across the street.

Three Men in a Tent

For Rufus C. Mitchell

My one blood-uncle laughs
and shakes his handsome head.
Yeah, that was Ol' Corbon.
He was your daddy's classmate,
you know: They went to school together
at Wilberforce.

Seemed like Ol' Corbon
was in trouble all the time.
We slept two guys to a tent,
you know, and seemed like nobody
wanted to bunk with Ol' Corbon.
He was such a hard-luck case;
the guys thought he was jinxed.

Finally, he came to me and Dillard
—Dillard was my tent-mate—
and asked if he could bunk with us,
because he knew your dad.
He said he'd sleep
at the foot of our tent.
Dillard said, *Shit, man,*
but I talked him over.

We were on Cape Bon, Tunisia,
you know, and we had to take turns
doing guard-duty.
The Germans parachuted soldiers in
almost every night,
and they knifed men
sleeping in their tents.

One night it was Ol' Corbon's turn,
and he fell asleep on duty.
You know,
you can be shot
for doing that in combat.
But Ol' Corbon bailed himself out;
he bought life
with his black mother-wit.

The water there
was corroding the cooling systems.
If they rusted too much,
the planes couldn't fly.
Most of the pilots

—Negro and white—
were just sitting around.
The ground-crews were going crazy,
but what could we do?
You had to use water,
and the corrosive water
was the only water we had.

Then Ol' Corbon remembered
that they'd had to build a distillery
to make distilled water
for the chemistry lab at Wilberforce.
Hey, man, he told me,
I think we can do that.
So we rag-patched one together
and got our boys
back in the air.

The Commanding Officer came over
to find out why the colored boys could fly,
and Ol' Corbon explained our distillery.

Then there were the spark-plug cleaners.
You know, it's easy in the States
to clean spark plugs:
you just use a spark-plug cleaner.
But we didn't have spark-plug cleaners;
they were back in the States.
The planes were grounded again
while we waited.
Thirty to sixty days,
they said it would take.

But Ol' Corbon said
Hey, man,
I bet we can make one.
You want to try?

Well, it turns out
to be pretty simple
to make a spark-plug cleaner.
You just take a big can,
fill it with desert sand,
make a space at the top
for a spark plug,

and blast high-pressure air
through a hole in the side.

You know, the first time
I saw General Eisenhower
was when he flew in
to find out why
the 99th was flying.

The CO introduced Staff Sergeant Corbon.

A little while later
Cape Bon Airfield
was integrated.
We were five men to a tent:
one of us
to four
of them.

I sure missed
my old buddies.
I even missed
Ol' Corbon.

Lonely Eagles

For Daniel "Chappie" James, General USAF
and for the 332nd Fighter Group

Being black in America
was the Original Catch,
so no one was surprised
by 22:
The segregated airstrips,
separate camps.
They did the jobs
they'd been trained to do.

Black ground-crews kept them in the air;
black flight-surgeons kept them alive;
the whole Group removed their headgear
when another pilot died.

They were known by their names:
"Ace" and "Lucky,"
"Sky-hawk Johnny," "Mr. Death."
And by their positions and planes.
Red Leader to Yellow Wing-man,
do you copy?

If you could find a fresh egg
you bought it and hid it
in your dopp-kit or your boot
until you could eat it alone.
On the night before a mission
you gave a buddy
your hiding-places
as solemnly
as a man dictating
his will.
There's a chocolate bar
in my Bible;
my whiskey bottle
is inside my bed-roll.

In beat-up Flying Tigers
that had seen action in Burma,
they shot down three German jets.
They were the only outfit
in the American Air Corps
to sink a destroyer
with fighter planes.
Fighter planes with names
like "By Request."

Sometimes the radios
didn't even work.

They called themselves
"Hell from Heaven."
This Spookwaffe.
My father's old friends.

It was always
maximum effort:
A whole squadron
of brother-men
raced across the tarmac
and mounted their planes.

>   My tent-mate was a guy named Starks.
>   The funny thing about me and Starks
>   was that my air mattress leaked,
>   and Starks' didn't.
>   Every time we went up,
>   I gave my mattress to Starks
>   and put his on my cot.

>   One day we were strafing a train.
>   Strafing's bad news:
>   you have to fly so low and slow
>   you're a pretty clear target.
>   My other wing-man and I
>   exhausted our ammunition and got out.
>   I recognized Starks
>   by his red tail
>   and his rudder's trim-tabs.
>   He couldn't pull up his nose.
>   He dived into the train
>   and bought the farm.

>   I found his chocolate,
>   three eggs, and a full fifth
>   of his hoarded-up whiskey.
>   I used his mattress
>   for the rest of my tour.

>   It still bothers me, sometimes:
>   I was sleeping
>   on his breath.

Star-Fix

For Melvin M. Nelson, Captain USAF (ret.)
(1917–1966)

At his cramped desk
under the astrodome,
the navigator looks
thousands of light-years
everywhere but down.
He gets a celestial fix,
measuring head-winds;
checking the log;
plotting wind-speed,
altitude, drift
in a circle of protractors,
slide-rules, and pencils.

He charts in his Howgozit
the points of no alternate
and of no return.
He keeps his eyes on the compass,
the two altimeters, the map.
He thinks, *Do we have enough fuel?*
What if my radio fails?

He's the only Negro in the crew.
The only black flyer on the whole base,
for that matter. Not that it does:
this crew is a team.
Bob and Al, Les, Smitty, Nelson.

Smitty, who said once
after a poker game,
I love you, Nelson.
I never thought I could love
a colored man.
When we get out of this man's Air Force,
if you ever come down to Tuscaloosa,
look me up and come to dinner.
You can come in the front door, too;
hell, you can stay overnight!
Of course, as soon as you leave,
I'll have to burn down my house.
Because if I don't
my neighbors will.

The navigator knows where he is
because he knows where he's been
and where he's going.

At night, since he can't fly
by dead-reckoning,
he calculates his position
by shooting a star.

The octant tells him
the angle of a fixed star
over the artificial horizon.
His position in that angle
is absolute and true:
Where the hell are we, Nelson?
Alioth, in the Big Dipper.
Regulus. Antares, in Scorpio.

He plots their lines
of position on the chart,
gets his radio bearing,
corrects for lost time.

Bob, Al, Les, and Smitty
are counting on their navigator.
If he sleeps,
they all sleep.
If he fails
they fall.

The navigator keeps watch
over the night and the instruments,
going hungry for five or six hours
to give his flight-lunch
to his two little girls.

Porter

For Bertram Wilson, Lieutenant Colonel USAF (ret.)
and for all of my "uncles"

Suddenly
when I hear airplanes overhead—
big, silver ones
whose muscles fill the sky—
I listen: That sounds like
someone I know.
And the sky
looks much closer.

I know my intimacy, now,
with the wheel and roar
of wind around wings.
Hello, wind.
Take care of my people.
The moon and stars
aren't so white now;
some of my people
know their first names.
Hey, Arcturus.
What's happening, Polaris?
Daddy said I should look you up.

You're even
more
dumb-founding
than he told me you were.

This is my other heritage:
I have roots in the sky.
The Tuskegee Airmen
are my second family.
This new, brave,
decorated tribe.

My family.
My homeplace, at last.
It was there
all through time.
I only had
to raise my eyes.

Tuskegee Airmen,
uncles of my childhood,
how shall I live and work
to match your goodness?
Can I do more

than murmur name upon name,
as the daughter
of a thousand proud fathers?

Jefferson.
Wilson.
Sparks.
Toliver.
Woodward.
Mitchell.
Price.
Lacy.
Straker.
Smith.
Washington.
Meriweather.
White . . .

> One time, this was in the Sixties,
> and I was a full-bird Colonel,
> they called me in Kentucky
> and asked me to pick up
> an aircraft somebody had crashed
> down in Louisiana.
> I was supposed to fly it
> to a base in New Mexico
> and go back to Kentucky
> on a commercial flight.
>
> It's tricky business,
> flying a plane that's been crashed.
> You can never tell
> what might still be wrong with it.
>
> Okay, I flew the plane to New Mexico
> and got on a flight back home.
> I was in full dress-uniform,
> decorations and medals
> and shit
> all over my chest.
> The Distinguished Flying Cross
> with two Bronze Oak Leaf Clusters,
> The Bronze Star,
> a couple of commendation medals,
> a European-African-Middle East Campaign Medal
> with four Bronze Service Stars . . .

When we landed in Chicago
I was standing in the aisle
when a lady—
a little grayhaired white lady—
asked me to lift
her suitcase down.
I said, *Of course,*
and carried it on out
into the terminal for her.
When I put it down
she handed me a dime
as a tip.

He looks down.
Then he looks at me and grins.

   I TOOK it, too!